Publisher: W. Quay Hays
Editorial Director: Peter L. Hoffman
Production Director: Trudihope Schlomowitz
Prepress Manager: Bill Castillo
Copy Editor: Amy Spitalnick
Production Artists: Robert Avellan, Dave Chadderdon, Gus Dawson, Gaston Moraga, Maritta Tapanainen, Regina Troyer
Production Assistant: Tom Archibeque

For information:
General Publishing Group, Inc.
2701 Ocean Park Boulevard
Santa Monica, California 90405

Library of Congress Cataloging-in-Publication Data

Nesheim, Eric.
     Saucer attack! / created and designed by Eric Nesheim ; written by
Eric and Leif Nesheim.
       p. cm.
     ISBN 1-57544-066-0
     1. Unidentified flying objects--Popular works. I. Nesheim, Leif.
II. Title.
TL789.N47 1997
001.942--dc21

97-22098
CIP

Printed by RR Donnelley & Sons, Inc. in Mexico
10 9 8 7 6 5 4 3 2 1

A Kitchen Sink Press book for
General Publishing Group, Inc.
Los Angeles

SAUCER ATTACK!

created and designed by ERIC NESHEIM

written by ERIC *and* LEIF NESHEIM

**A KITCHEN SINK PRESS book for
GENERAL PUBLISHING GROUP, INC.**
Los Angeles, CA

C O N T E N T S

Flying saucers invaded the decorative arts of the 1950s as exemplified by this border...

CONTENTS

...by noted saucer illustrator Alex Schomburg. It originally appeared in WONDER STORY ANNUAL.

FLYING WHAT?

IT IS A SUMMER MORNING, early 1950s. A man drives his wife and two small children home from church through a quiet neighborhood in Marion, Indiana. Suddenly, high overhead, he spots dozens of small, silvery discs fluttering slowly to Earth. He runs his car into the curb, leaps out, and abandoning his family, goes shouting down the street: "THEY'RE HERE! THE SAUCERS ARE LANDING! THEY'RE HERE!" When no one responds, the man starts pounding on people's doors. Still in the car, his mortified wife can only crouch down in the seat. People finally begin to gather, wondering what the shouting is all about. At the same time, the discs start to hit the ground all around. Someone picks one up and says: "Hey, buddy, look. Pie plates with printin' on 'em. Musta dropped from a plane." The man who saw the saucers was my father. He won't admit it, and I don't remember it, but my mother has made it a family legend—our small contribution to the saucer craze.

SAUCERS CAME INTO the public psyche at a time of great tension and paranoia in America. People feared "the Bomb" and communist infiltration. The Korean war, Sputnik, and our early failures in the space race had shaken national confidence. I recall being sprayed by a tobacco-chewing neighbor when he excitedly told me how Khrushchev and the "Russkies" were going to take us over without

Paul Lindberg's FLYING SAUCER was the first plastic flying saucer model kit. It was manufactured in Skokie, Illinois, in the early 1950s.

6

even firing a shot. Carl Jung believed that flying saucers were psychological projections of cultural fears and desires in an uncertain world. Substituting the words "communist infiltrator" for the words "flying saucer" in some early saucer books seems to bear this out.

FOLLOWING JUNG'S LEAD, critics have suggested that movies like *Earth Vs. The Flying Saucers* (1956) and *Invasion of the Body Snatchers* (1956) are political allegories or metaphors for cultural tensions. But as a kid who grew up in the '50s, I just thought saucer movies were cool! A favorite of mine was *The Mysterians* (*Chikyu Boeigun,* 1957). It had everything: flying saucers, evil aliens, abducted women, and army guys fighting giant, city-stomping robots! Much of my play unconsciously followed *The Mysterians'* plot or those of kindred films and comic books. Many toys available in the late '50s and early '60s were similar to the film's major elements. I used toy soldiers, space ships, and my giant Robot Commando to endlessly reenact scenarios like those in the movie.

THE PUBLIC FIRST became aware of flying saucers when the press reported Kenneth Arnold's now famous sighting in June 1947. By 1950, the first round of saucer books were out and a film linking Russians and saucers entitled *The Flying Saucer* (1950) had been released. By mid-decade, George Adamski and Buck Nelson had told of their contacts with saucer people. By 1956, most of the best saucer films had been produced. And by the late '50s, flying saucers had invaded practically every aspect of popular

IS THIS TOMORROW's (1947) graphic depictions of lynchings and executions alerted Catholic kids to the menace of communism—and no doubt caused many to lose sleep as well. Over four million copies of this Catechetical Guild comic book were distributed, a major contribution to postwar paranoia.

Also contributing to sleeplessness, a school-distributed Civil Defense pamphlet (1956).

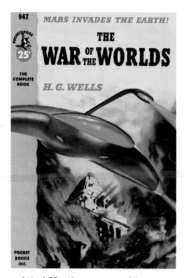

An updated Martian war machine turns Los Angeles into Hiroshima, U.S.A., on the cover of the Pocket Book edition of THE WAR OF THE WORLDS, concurrently released with George Pal's 1953 film production.

culture. Common objects, from salt and pepper shakers to coffee mugs, boasted saucer motifs. Several popular songs featured saucers. Numerous toys had saucer themes, and bubble gum cards displayed lurid saucer images. Flying saucers became as much a convention in comic books as balloon-muscled heroes in tights.

THIS BOOK examines the artifacts and images of the Golden Age of flying saucers. It contains popular illustrations of saucers, weird aliens, space invasions, and related esoterica from movie posters, books, magazines, toys, and artifacts. These depictions of flying saucers are the products of the time in which they were created. As metaphors for the hopes and fears of an era, they can tell us something about ourselves. And this, more than proving the reality of flying saucers, is perhaps the most important aspect of the phenomenon….Watch out for those pie plates!

—ERIC NESHEIM
June 1997, Madison, Wisconsin

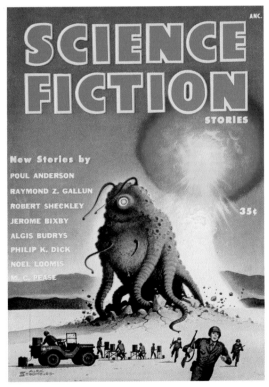

Marx toy soldiers battle valiantly for Earth upon a distant asteroid…or maybe it was the linoleum floor in my parents' suburban home—a vision from my youth (above) inspired by THE MYSTERIANS (1959; press book image, opposite bottom). Nuclear destruction was a recurrent theme in movies and books of the '50s. SCIENCE FICTION STORIES' cover (no.1, '53, left) expressed a common apprehension of the era: to unlock the mysteries of the atom was to open a modern Pandora's box.

ORSON WELLES'
WAR OF THE WORLDS

The Actual Broadcast by The Mercury Theatre on the Air as heard over the Columbia Broadcasting System, October 30, 1938. The most thrilling drama ever broadcast from the famed HOWARD KOCH script!

Man Wants to Fight Ma

Causes Variety of

FAKE RADIO 'WAR STIRS TERRO

An authentic first edition...

INVASION FROM MARS

Hadley Cantril

IDY IN THE PSYCHOLOGY OF PANIC

BRITS WHO READ *The War of the Worlds* when it was first published discovered what being on the other side of imperial conquest was like. The British Empire's Maxim guns, effective against indigenous natives, were no match for the Martians' heat ray. In H. G. Wells's story (serialized in *The Cosmopolitan,* 1897), invading Martians crush Victorian England before being done in by the sniffles. *The War of the Worlds* is generally considered to be the first alien invasion novel. It has been reprinted numerous times, providing a template for perhaps thousands of similar stories. It has appeared in practically every medium, notably in Orson Welles's 1938 radio broadcast.

"Across the gulf of space…intellects vast and cool and unsympathetic, regarded this earth with envious eyes."
—THE WAR OF THE WORLDS, 1897.

ON HALLOWEEN night in 1938, thousands of Americans were panicked to the point of hysteria by Orson Welles's radio dramatization of *The War of the Worlds*. According to newspapers, a "tidal wave of terror" swept the East Coast. People hearing the broadcast believed an actual invasion from Mars was being reported, that unstoppable monsters were burning their way across the nation. Many behaved as if the end of the world was at hand—some ran amok, others fainted or tried to hide. One man overturned his car in a wild dash while another returned home to find his wife clutching a bottle of poison. In 1950, Donald Keyhoe (*The Flying Saucers Are Real*) suspected that the government feared a similar mass hysteria if the truth about flying saucers were made public. Keyhoe's own beliefs were shaken by the saucer reports he had investigated. He feared that saucer occupants, like H. G. Wells's Martians, would view us as primitives. And, if the public was not prepared, contact with a superior race would throw it into panic.

A Martian as depicted by Warwick Goble for "The War of the Worlds" in the November 1897, issue of THE COSMOPOLITAN (above). To cash in on the radio show's furor, Dell hastily released a cheap edition of THE WAR OF THE WORLDS (1938, opposite). Printed on stock approximating thick toilet paper, few intact copies exist. Those that do are usually torn and tattered.

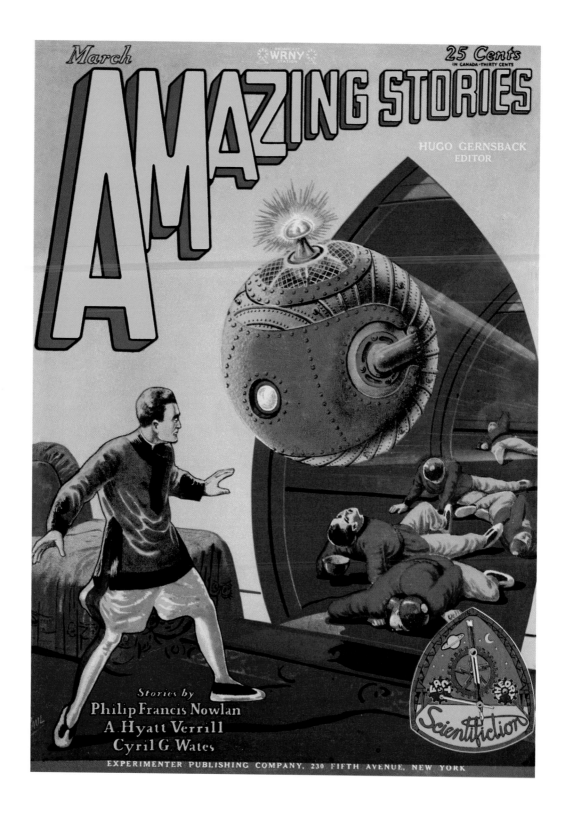

"ARMAGEDDON-2419 A.D." and its sequel "The Airlords of Han" (*Amazing Stories*, Aug. '28 and March '29), by Philip Francis Nowlan, were the basis of the seminal *Buck Rogers* comic strip. Drawn by Dick Calkins the strip was noted for its fanciful space ships, like the mysterious saucer in "The Tiger Men of Mars" (no. 384, '30, right). The cover illustration for the "Airlords of Han" (opposite) by Frank R. Paul features a gravity-defying UFO. Both illustrations predate the '50s saucer craze by almost 20 years.

The Buck Rogers Flying Saucer (above) is likely a '50s toy. The 1938 patent refers to the registration date of the paper plate the saucer is printed on. The toy space ships (above right) are Buck Rogers Popsicle Premiums from the late '30s.

UPON THE TELESCOPE VIEWPLATE, APPEARED THE HULK OF A STRANGE SPACE CRAFT – BUT IT WAS **NOT** A MARTIAN VESSEL –

DICK CALKINS
384
TO BE CONTINUED

There'll be nothing left to see if every tourist takes a souvenir—SCIENCE WONDER STORIES (Nov. '29).

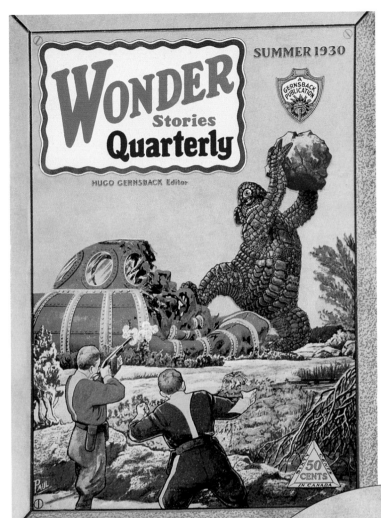

Images resembling flying saucers and UFOs adorned the covers of early science fiction magazines well in advance of the '50s saucer craze. The shoe is on the other foot (left) when a monster smashes the saucer of invading Earthmen (WONDER STORIES QUARTERLY, summer '30). Below is a detail of a Leo Morey illustration (AMAZING STORIES, March '35). Above is a depiction of an actual UFO sighted in 1910 (AMAZING STORIES, Jan. '48).

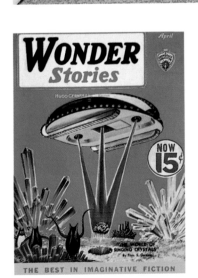

WONDER STORIES, April 1936.

The Golden Age of flying saucers began with Kenneth Arnold's (right) famous sighting, shown on the cover of FATE's first issue (spring '48, opposite). With the help of FATE publisher Ray Palmer, Arnold retold his story in THE COMING OF THE SAUCERS (1952, below).

The COMING of the SAUCERS

$2.50

By Kenneth Arnold & Ray Palmer

LIKE A FLYING SAUCER

ON JUNE 25, 1947, newspaper reporter Bill Bequette (*East Oregonian,* Pendleton, Oregon) coined the term "flying saucer" to describe what pilot Kenneth Arnold had seen the previous day. An experienced mountain pilot, Arnold had been flying in the vicinity of Mt. Rainier, Washington. At 3 p.m. his eye was attracted to a series of flashes. He saw a formation of nine highly reflective flat objects traveling in the distant mountain tops. Arnold described their motion by saying "they flew like a saucer would if you skipped it across the water." To compute their speed, Arnold timed the objects as they zipped between Mts. Adams and Rainier, 20 miles ahead of his position. He assumed he had been watching a new kind of jet plane. But the speed he calculated, 1656.71 mph, far exceeded any aircraft at that time. Just one month prior to Arnold's sighting, *Mechanix Illustrated* had a cover story about the Navy's little-known, saucer-shaped, experimental airplane—the "flying Flapjack." Perhaps Arnold's, but more likely reporter Bequette's, denomination of flying saucer was influenced by the Flapjack feature. Arnold's sighting received unprecedented coverage, and suddenly people everywhere were observing flying "dimes," "hubcaps," and "ice cream cones" in the sky. This public furor prompted the Air Force to establish "Project Sign," or more popularly "Project Saucer," in December of 1947. Its mission was to assess the potential threat of flying saucers to national security. One month after the Mt. Rainier incident, Arnold investigated a saucer sighting near Tacoma for *Fate* publisher Ray Palmer. It became known as the Maury Island Hoax. En route, Arnold saw and attempted to film a flock of brass-colored flying objects that looked like ducks. Many UFOlogists cite Arnold's Mt. Rainier encounter as the beginning of the "modern age" of flying saucers.

FATE

VOLUME 1   NUMBER 1

SPRING
1948
25c

*Many Other Startling
Articles And Features*

The FLYING DISKS

RAY PALMER (1910-1977) greatly influenced the early years of flying saucers by popularizing the subject. The P.T. Barnum of saucers, Palmer's sensational reports kept the public interested while sustaining his eclectic publishing business. A controversial editor for *Amazing Stories*, Palmer quit in 1948 when his plans for an all-saucer issue met with resistance. He immediately started his own publication, *Fate*. The first issue featured Kenneth Arnold's famous sighting. Subsequent issues pandered to the early saucer fanatics. After selling his interest in *Fate*, Palmer published a bewildering array of books and magazines cut from the same cloth. In one, he claimed to have observed an orange globe hovering above his Amherst, Wisconsin, offices.

Palmer graces the cover of MYSTIC MAGAZINE (May '56, right), one of his own publications. In 1957, Palmer concentrated on publishing mostly saucer material. FLYING SAUCERS FROM OTHER WORLDS was the result. The magazine lasted into the 1960s as FLYING SAUCERS.

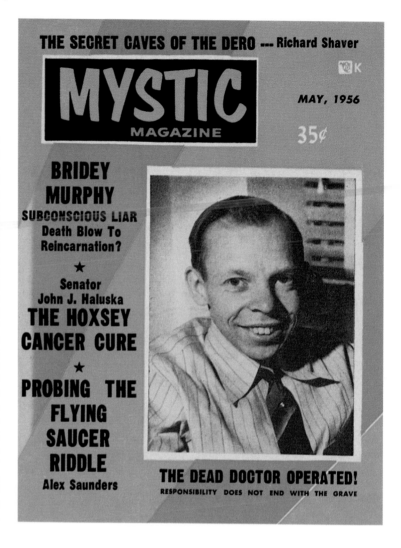

THE SECRET CAVES OF THE DERO --- Richard Shaver

MYSTIC MAGAZINE

MAY, 1956

35¢

BRIDEY MURPHY
SUBCONSCIOUS LIAR
Death Blow To Reincarnation?

★

Senator John J. Haluska
THE HOXSEY CANCER CURE

★

PROBING THE FLYING SAUCER RIDDLE
Alex Saunders

THE DEAD DOCTOR OPERATED!
RESPONSIBILITY DOES NOT END WITH THE GRAVE

Three Palmer publications: FLYING SAUCERS (Nov. '63), MYSTIC MAGAZINE (Jan. '54), and FLYING SAUCERS (July '62).

JUNE
35¢

FLYING SAUCERS
FROM OTHER WORLDS

FLYING SAUCER PILGRIMAGE

By Bryant & Helen Reeve

**The True Story of a 23,000 Mile Pursuit of Flying Saucers
and the People Who Have Contacted Them.**

ELIZABETH KLARER'S FLYING SAUCER ★ SAUCER OVER PARIS

South African Woman Sees and Photographs the Famous Disks

One of the Most Sensational
Sightings Recorded on Radar

SIGHTINGS BY SCIENTISTS ★ THE MAN WHO STARTED IT ALL

The May 1956 FATE reports on a telepathic experiment in Texas to attract saucers. It was witnessed by a local deputy sheriff. Barney to Mars...Barney to Mars...Over.

LONE STAR ENCOUNTERS

IN THE LATE EVENING of November 2, 1957, a spectacular series of sightings began in the Levelland, Texas, area. An excited Pedro Saucedo phoned the Levelland police station and reported that a huge torpedo-shaped craft had landed in a field west of town. It then rose up and sped directly toward his truck. The truck's lights and engine died as the ship roared overhead, shaking the truck. After the craft shot by, the truck's lights came back on. The officer who took the call dismissed it as drunken rambling, until he received another call: Jim Wheeler was driving east of town when he found the highway blocked by a similar object, emitting an intense, blinding glare. Wheeler's car also ceased to function. Five more almost identical encounters were reported over the next few hours, most along desolate roads. The last reported sightings were by the sheriff and other police officers who witnessed brilliant red lights above the highway. Although the incident made national headlines, the Air Force sent only one investigator. He spent less than 24 hours in Levelland, interviewing only six of the witnesses. The AF then issued a press release which claimed the sightings were nothing more than ball lightning. They blamed all the vehicle failures on wet electrical connections, even though the weather was dry and there were no storms in the area.

SAUCERS TRAIL AIRLINER

FATE
PDC
MAGAZINE

Interview with DONALD KEYHOE

August 1959 35c

KEEP YOUR EYE ON VENUS—Frank Edwards

FATE and other publications were quick to publish saucer reports of responsible witnesses. According to the August '59 FATE (opposite), Captain Peter W. Killian observed three glowing UFOs pace his plane. Killian and a nearby airline pilot took a bearing on the capering objects, computing a rough distance of 20 miles. The February '59 FATE (left) contains an article about four elliptical craft that repeatedly swooped over a train in central Indiana. A fictional collision —AMAZING STORIES' special FLYING SAUCER issue (Oct. '57, below).

Secretary of the Navy Daniel Kimball's 1952 saucer encounter, documented in EC Comics' WEIRD SCIENCE FANTASY (Dec. '54).

An overly optimistic rendering of the "Avrocar," a flying saucer developed in the '50s for the USAF by A.V. Roe of Canada (FATE, Oct. '53). Frisbees flew better! Santa must have gotten his "Avro" at a surplus sale (UNIVERSE, Jan. '55).

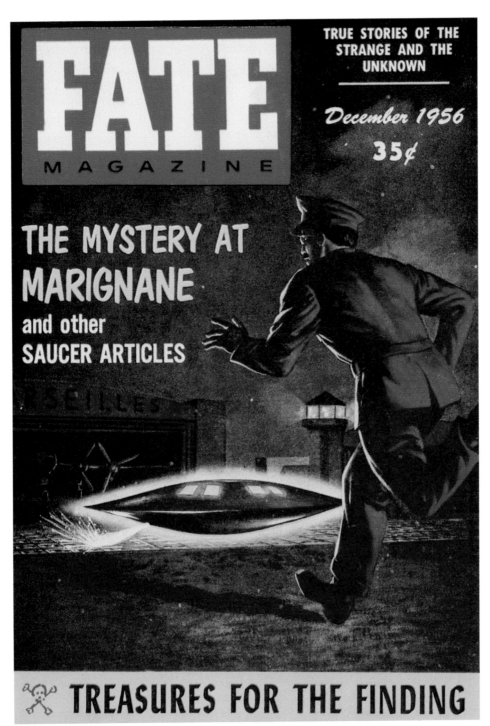

FATE regularly reprinted excerpts from saucer books. This December '56 FATE featured a French customs officer's close encounter, from Aime Michel's THE TRUTH ABOUT FLYING SAUCERS (1956).

Internationally respected astronomer Dr. Clyde Tombaugh, the discoverer of Pluto, reported seeing UFOs on several occasions. One sighting was documented in the Dec. 1952 FATE (right).

THE GLOWING FIREBALLS investigated by Project Twinkle stand out as one of the few UFO phenomena that investigators assumed to exist from the beginning. Almost everyone who was involved in the project personally witnessed the mysterious, luminescent objects—including noted scientists, trained pilots, and military personnel. What began with a few reports of "green flares" in New Mexico, 1949, soon became the subject of a full-fledged investigation. When the crews of an Air Force C-47 and a civilian DC-3 both reported huge, glowing, green meteors on a flat trajectory, Air Force personnel became concerned. The sightings were near a military installation which was conducting atomic tests. The University of New Mexico's Institute of Meteoritics Professor Dr. Lincoln La Paz was called in to investigate but was unable to find anything to indicate that the fireballs were meteors. For that reason Dr. La Paz led a faction of investigators who believed the fireballs were not natural. The suggested possibilities included the idea that they were remote-controlled saucers testing the Earth's atmosphere. An official committee considered Dr. La Paz's theories but ultimately decided that the fireballs were natural. Project Twinkle was given one of three requested cameras to document the fireballs but was unable to capture anything on film.

28

The June 1957 issue of FATE featured an excerpted chapter from Edward J. Ruppelt's book, THE REPORT ON FLY-ING SAUCERS (1956). It detailed his experience with Project Twinkle's green fireballs. As Ruppelt tells it, there were numerous other sightings and opportunities for investigating them. None were seriously acted upon and the press became uninterested.

This cover illustrates an occurrence excerpted from Ruppelt's book.
Several other incidents from THE REPORT ON UNIDENTIFIED
FLYING OBJECTS (1956) are also mentioned in the story.

At Last! Former Air Force Expert Reveals HUSHED-UP FACTS ON "FLYING SAUCERS"

★ ★ ★ The only book about FLYING SAUCERS based entirely on OFFICIAL AIR FORCE RECORDS

ACE
DOUBLE SIZE
BOOKS
D-200

35¢

THE REPORT ON

UNIDENTIFIED

FLYING

OBJECTS

EDWARD J. RUPPELT
Former Head of the United States Air Force Project Investigating Flying Saucers

Complete & Unabridged

THE REPORT ON UNIDENTIFIED FLYING OBJECTS

Edward

NOT fiction but thought-provoking FACT by the former head of the U. S. Air Force PROJECT BLUE BOOK investigating "Flying Saucers."

(Above) The first chief of Project Blue Book, Captain Edward J. Ruppelt, writes about his experiences and some of the cases he encountered during his tenure from early 1951 to Sept. 1953. An ad for Ruppelt's book appears on the back of VENTURE (March 1957, top).

The Air Force spared no expense in funding the crack Project Blue Book team—note the high-tech charts. The entire ace team (shown here in LOOK magazine's special issue, FLYING SAUCERS, 1967) was head-quartered in an 18 by 30 foot room through the '50s and '60s. You can sleep well at night knowing they're on the job!

Frank Scully's book BEHIND THE FLYING SAUCERS (1951) contains a fantastic report about three crashed saucers and the small, dead occupants within. The only problem: Scully's chief source, the enigmatic "Dr. Gee," was a TV repairman later convicted on charges of operating a confidence game. By then, Scully's book had already sold more than 60,000 copies, so it didn't really matter.

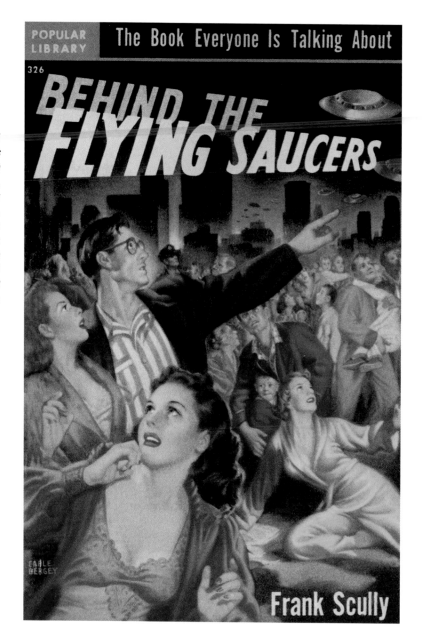

THE FLYING SAUCERS ARE REAL (1950) by Donald Keyhoe is an expanded version of a magazine article of his. A primer of classic saucer dogma and paranoia, it contains phrases like "saucer scare" and "interplanetary spies," reminiscent of Cold War jargon. Keyhoe dictums: Saucers might be U.S. or Russian secret weapons; the government was hiding the truth; saucer surveillance increased after A-bomb tests; saucers were interplanetary craft.

Three classics from the Golden Age of flying saucers: FLYING SAUCERS FROM OUTER SPACE (1953), THE FLYING SAUCER CONSPIRACY (1955), FLYING SAUCERS–TOP SECRET (1960). All are by Donald Keyhoe (1897–1988). Keyhoe, a retired Marine Major, had several high-ranking friends in the government and military. Consequently, his books contained much "inside" information. Some UFO researchers believe Keyhoe was deliberately fed misinformation.

FLYING SAUCERS

from

outer space

Major DONALD E. KEYHOE
U.S. MARINE CORPS (ret.)

IMPORTANT: SEE BACK OF JACKET

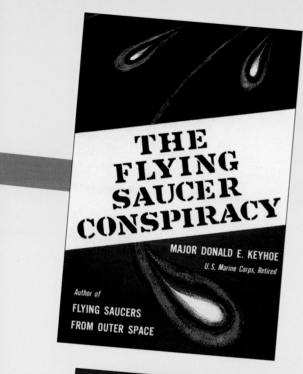

MOMENT OF SILENCE

DONALD KEYHOE BECAME a focal point of the UFO phenomenon in 1950 when he accused the U.S. government of covering up vital saucer information. In his article "The Flying Saucers Are Real," for *True* (Jan. '50), Keyhoe claimed the government feared panic if the truth about saucers were known. The article caused a sensation upon its release. Newspapers and radio stations picked up the story and *True* was flooded with letters. In 1957, Keyhoe became head of the National Investigations Committee on Aerial Phenomenon (NICAP). In 1958, he appeared on a television program about flying saucers. The lone saucer supporter, he was exasperated with the heavy editing of his script by Air Force officials. When he began to disclose information not cleared by the AF, his voice was cut off the air, ostensibly for reasons of national security. Years later, Keyhoe concocted a scheme to contact space aliens called "Operation Lure." The idea was to attract UFOs to land by baiting selected areas with dummy flying saucers.

TV viewers fiddled with the sound on their sets, not realizing that Donald Keyhoe's voice had been deliberately cut off.

A MIB BEHIND EVERY BUSH!

With chapter titles like 'Capture of the Innocents' and 'Clear and Present Danger,' MEN WITHOUT FACES (1950, opposite) could have inspired the paranoia in Gray Barker's THEY KNEW TOO MUCH ABOUT FLYING SAUCERS (1956). In it Barker (above) writes: "One by one, the leading figures among flying saucer researchers, who have challenged the government denial that saucers come from outerspace, have been silenced."

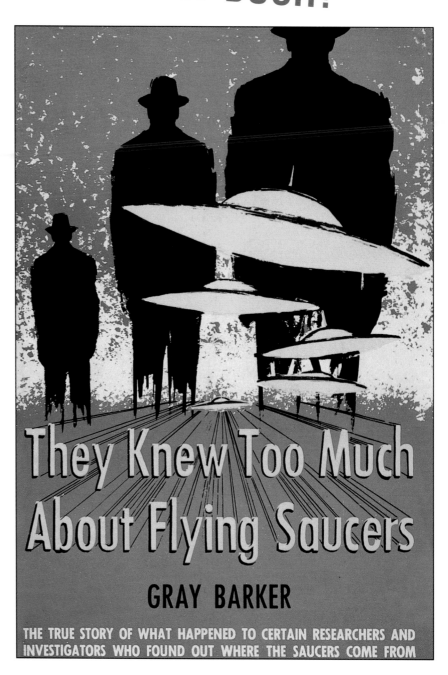

They Knew Too Much About Flying Saucers

GRAY BARKER

THE TRUE STORY OF WHAT HAPPENED TO CERTAIN RESEARCHERS AND INVESTIGATORS WHO FOUND OUT WHERE THE SAUCERS COME FROM

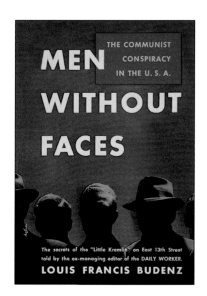

THE COMMUNIST
CONSPIRACY
IN THE U. S. A.

MEN
WITHOUT
FACES

The secrets of the "Little Kremlin" on East 13th Street
told by the ex-managing editor of the DAILY WORKER.
LOUIS FRANCIS BUDENZ

"JUST BEFORE the men left one of them said, 'I suppose you know you're on your honor as an American. If I hear another word out of your office you're in trouble.'" This quote, from Gray Barker's book *They Knew Too Much About Flying Saucers*, is very similar to the anti-communist propaganda in *Men Without Faces*. Both books portray the enemy as an insidious force that utilizes secretive and devious methods of control and intimidation. Barker's book refers to the alleged silencing of saucer researchers by mysterious "Men [dressed] In Black." It is one of saucerdom's first treatments of the MIB—strange people who dress in out-of-date clothes and intimidate UFO witnesses. Some believe the MIB are government agents, others think they are aliens from another world. In one MIB incident, victim George Cook's neighbor witnessed three strange men, who had visited Cook earlier, shove him into a car equipped with fake plates. Cook, head of a local saucer group, later claimed to have vague recollections of being forced aboard a flying saucer. Yikes!

"The Truth of the Existence of Flying Saucers Cannot Be Censored."
—FLYING SAUCERS UNCENSORED (1955).

"Did the 'flying saucers' come to help us or harm us?"
—advertisement for THE CASE FOR THE UFO (1955).

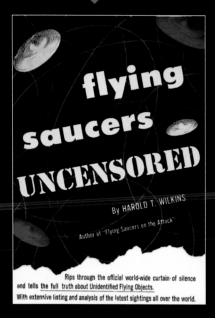

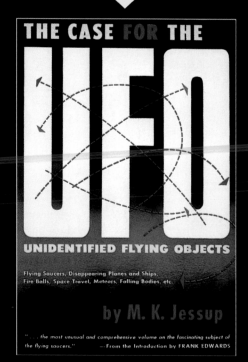

"The earth is already engaged in interplanetary warfare."—THE EXPANDING CASE FOR THE UFO (1957).

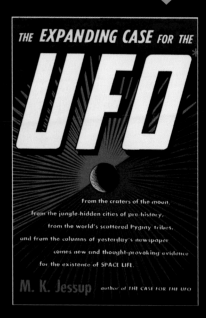

"HAS THE INVASION of Earth by beings from another world already begun?" In answer, Harold T. Wilkins reports numerous saucer hostilities in *Flying Saucers on the Attack* (1954). He contends in one chapter that Captain Thomas Mantell (the first person to die chasing a UFO) was shot down by a "Colossal Death Ray Aeroform." In *Flying Saucers Uncensored* (1955), Wilkins alleges official suppression of saucer information, the "Hush-Hush conspiracy." Donald Keyhoe's concurrent book *The Flying Saucer Conspiracy* (1955) also mentions a "silence group." "Have the Russians captured a space ship? Or have the space people taken over the Red Empire?" queries Morris K. Jessup in *The Case for the UFO* (1955). Jessup's controversial book became noted for its link to the "Allende letters," which tell of an incredible Navy experiment in teleportation during World War II.

flying saucers on the ATTACK

Startling *new* revelations on the most incredible story of our age!

by HAROLD T. WILKINS

George Adamski

GEORGE ADAMSKI (1891–1965) was among the first to claim regular contact with saucer occupants. He reported seeing a flying saucer in 1946 and later a huge fleet of saucers over Mt. Palomar. In 1952, Adamski had his first alleged encounter with saucer people. He reported subsequent contacts with numerous space persons: Firkon, a Martian; Ramu, a Saturnian; and many beautiful space women. Adamski claimed these aliens took him, by saucer, to visit their various home planets. A self-proclaimed "professor" and former fry-cook, Adamski somehow managed to cash in on his alleged experiences. He was sought after for lectures and for radio and TV appearances, and his books Flying Saucers Have Landed (1953) and Inside the Space Ships (1955) saw several editions. Adamski's stories and out-of-focus photos were all debunked, yet among saucerdom's fringe his influence persists.

Flying Saucers Have Landed

Desmond Leslie & George Adamski

George Adamski's alleged contacts with space people are chronicled in FLYING SAUCERS HAVE LANDED (1953).

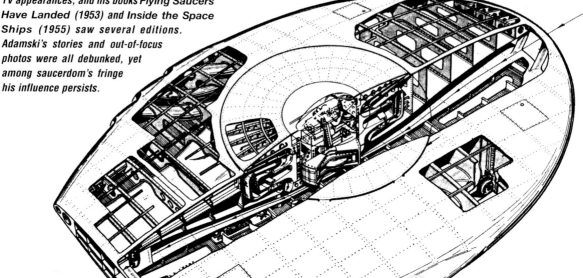

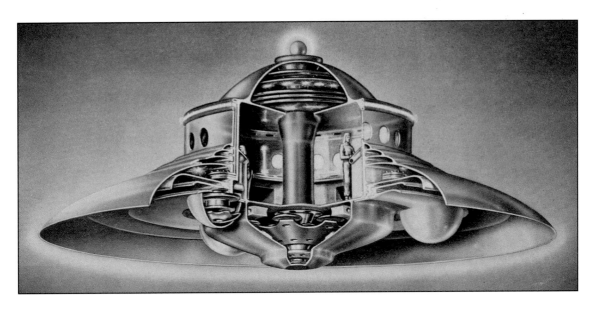

Introduction by Desmond Leslie

LEONARD G. CRAMP

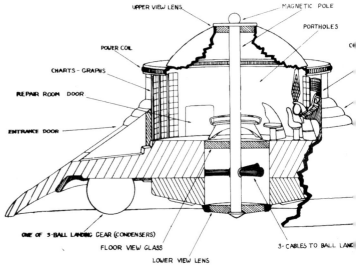

UPPER VIEW LENS

MAGNETIC POLE

PORTHOLES

POWER COIL

CHARTS - GRAPHS

REPAIR ROOM DOOR

ENTRANCE DOOR

ONE OF 3-BALL LANDING GEAR (CONDENSERS)

FLOOR VIEW GLASS

3 - CABLES TO BALL LAND

LOWER VIEW LENS

VENUSIAN SCOUT SHIP

SPACE, GRAVITY AND THE FLYING SAUCER (1955, left) by Leonard G. Cramp purports to be a serious scientific study of flying saucers. It contains drawings by the author of the A.V. Roe saucer (opposite) and Adamski's Venusian scout ship (top). A scout ship is also diagramed (above) in Adamski's INSIDE THE SPACE SHIPS (1955).

"I COULDN'T SEE THE SUN BECAUSE IT WAS VERY DARK IN SPACE."

PORTRAITS OF THE DEAD — Traver Bornholz

Search MAGAZINE

35¢

DECEMBER, 1956

FORMERLY **MYSTIC**

EISENHOWER'S HANDWRITING SHOWS CHANGED MAN
★
HOW TO MAKE SUPERSTITION WORK FOR YOU
★
ASTROLOGY AND E. S. P.
★
YOUR FUTURE
★
I VISITED MARS, VENUS and the MOON!
By Buck Nelson

AFTER GEORGE ADAMSKI'S success, contactees began to crawl out of the woodwork. The majority of saucer books published from 1954 through 1956 were contactee books. Akin to Biblical prophets, contactees claimed to have been selected by benevolent space people to relate messages of solace and reassurance. Buck Nelson's testimonial is typical of the early contactee. In 1955, Nelson, an Ozark Mountain farmer, claimed that he was taken for a ride by the occupants of a flying saucer. Of his space flight, Buck said: "I couldn't see the sun because it was very dark in space." The Saucer People allowed Buck to take a snapshot of their traveling companion: a giant telepathic Venusian dog, which looked amazingly like an ordinary

Buck Nelson tells how friendly space people took him for a spin around the planets in Ray Palmer's SEARCH MAGAZINE (Dec. '56, opposite right). Buck as he appeared IN LOOK magazine's special FLYING SAUCERS issue (1967, opposite left), which misnamed him "Duck Nelson." Buck and telepathic Venusian traveling companion (left). Inspired by the likes of George Adamski, Truman Bethurum, and other saucer luminaries, Bryant and Helen Reeve sold their house in 1954, bought a new car, weighted it down with saucer books, and embarked upon a three-year odyssey. Motoring across the U.S. and Mexico, they visited and usually wound up living with any contactee foolish enough to open the door. OK, they probably didn't stay all that long at Buck Nelson's. FLYING SAUCER PILGRIMAGE (1957, bottom right) is their story.

Flying Saucer Pilgrimage

Bryant & Helen Reeve

farm dog (the Aug. '47 issue of *Astounding Science Fiction* features a story about a space dog named Buck—hmm?). Nelson said that the Saucer People had given him information concerning solutions to Earth's problems. But, he added, "I can't pass it on yet. We are not ready for it." He was, however, able to share a recorded Christmas message from one of the Saucer People named, coincidentally, Bucky or Buck Jr. The message warned that our A-bombs were melting the Earth's ice caps and that America and all the world would be destroyed unless atomic weapons and warfare were abandoned. "We are here to see which way the world will use atomic power, for peace or for war. We wonder, and watch, and wait!"

S.RUDE '91

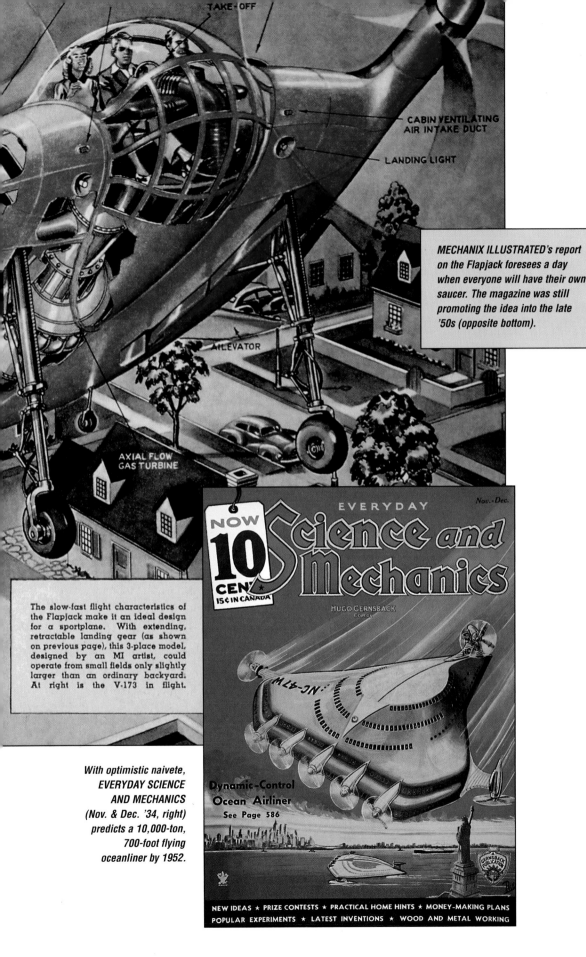

TAKE-OFF

CABIN VENTILATING
AIR INTAKE DUCT

LANDING LIGHT

AILEVATOR

AXIAL FLOW
GAS TURBINE

MECHANIX ILLUSTRATED's report on the Flapjack foresees a day when everyone will have their own saucer. The magazine was still promoting the idea into the late '50s (opposite bottom).

The slow-fast flight characteristics of the Flapjack make it an ideal design for a sportplane. With extending, retractable landing gear (as shown on previous page), this 3-place model, designed by an MI artist, could operate from small fields only slightly larger than an ordinary backyard. At right is the V-173 in flight.

With optimistic naivete, EVERYDAY SCIENCE AND MECHANICS (Nov. & Dec. '34, right) predicts a 10,000-ton, 700-foot flying oceanliner by 1952.

Nov.-Dec.

NOW 10 CENTS 15¢ IN CANADA

EVERYDAY
Science and Mechanics

HUGO GERNSBACK
EDITOR

NC-47W

Dynamic-Control
Ocean Airliner
See Page 586

NEW IDEAS ★ PRIZE CONTESTS ★ PRACTICAL HOME HINTS ★ MONEY-MAKING PLANS
POPULAR EXPERIMENTS ★ LATEST INVENTIONS ★ WOOD AND METAL WORKING

How The Flying Saucer Works

If you haven't seen saucers yet, you will—and they'll be built to Air Force specifications.

By Willy Ley

TOM McCAHILL REVIEWS HIS TEN YEARS OF CAR-TESTING

MECHANIX ILLUSTRATED

THE HOW-TO-DO MAGAZINE

25¢
MARCH

U. S. AIR FORCE REVEALS OUR FLYING SAUCER

BURIED GOLD IN LOUISIANA • THE WORLD'S MOST FABULOUS GUN

A LOOK INTO THE FUTURE of commercial aviation, where saucers may be the answer to airport congestion in *Mechanix Illustrated* (March '56, above). The magazine gives a brief and optimistic description of how the Air Force's A.V. Roe saucer would work by utilizing the "Coanda effect" (opposite).

A HUGE, low-flying UFO swept over the outskirts of Albuquerque, New Mexico, in 1951. An Atomic Energy Commission executive and his wife witnessed the craft from their yard. Their description of a fuselage-less, "wing-shaped" object also describes the Northrup Flying Wing; it first flew on June 25, 1946. Prop and jet versions were built. Production ceased in 1949 partly because of stability problems. Only three full-sized craft were produced, making the Flying Wing less likely to be seen over a backyard than an alien saucer.

The futuristic Flying Wing was a favorite with the kids of the '50s. The George Zaffo illustration (right) is from THE BIG BOOK OF REAL AIRPLANES (1951). The Apco paper glider (late '50s, below) was a gas station giveaway. "Designed as a practical approach to some of tomorrow's transportation problems—the Air Bus" is another overly optimistic saucer "solution"—SCIENCE AND MECHANICS (Dec. '50, opposite).

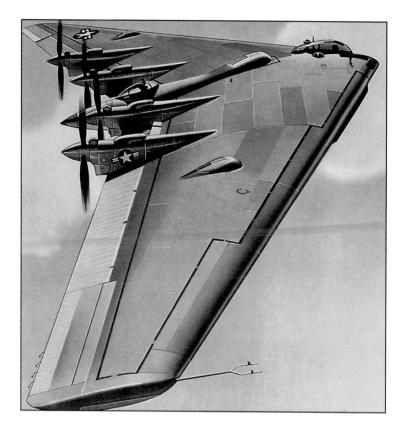

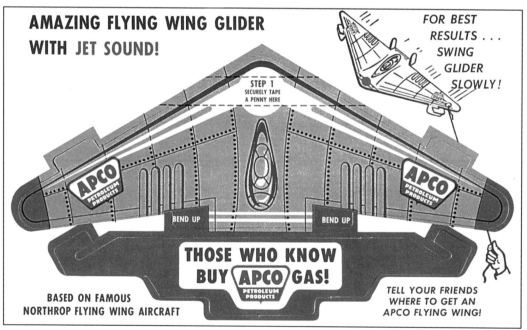

Galaxy
SCIENCE FICTION
AUGUST 1952
35¢

ANC

"The 40 Credit Tour of Earth" (GALAXY, Aug. '52, above). Earth doesn't hold a monopoly on Christmas, either; GALAXY (Jan. '58, right).

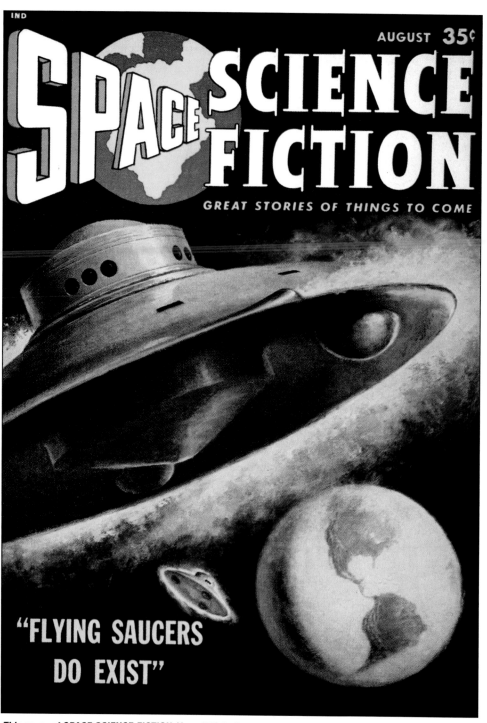

This cover of SPACE SCIENCE FICTION (Aug. '57) features a saucer based on George Adamski's description of the scout ships housed in the interplanetary Venusian motherships he was acquainted with.

MOTHERSHIPS

"HE SHOOK HIS head in the negative and made me understand that this craft had been brought into Earth's atmosphere in a larger ship…. So I asked if the large craft might be called a 'Mother' ship"—*Flying Saucers Have Landed* (1953). George Adamski coined the phrase "mothership" in reference to the large ships which carried the smaller scout ships into the Earth's atmosphere. This idea has been adopted by other saucer theorists, some of whom suggest that the scouts may be remote-controlled drones.

OTHERWORLDS SCIENCE STORIES (March '52, left). FATE (March '55, below). Cigar-shaped saucer images.

One of Adamski's 1951 telescope photos, allegedly of a mothership releasing scouts—INSIDE THE SPACE SHIPS (1955, above).

CRASH!!!

"NO, WE DON'T have any little bodies in our cellar. It's impossible. We don't have a cellar!"—Major Hector Quintanilla, Project Blue Book. In 1949 and '50, wire services carried serious yet unsubstantiated accounts of crashed saucers yielding heaps of dead "little men." Frank Scully's book, *Behind the Flying Saucers* (1951), added to the alleged body count. One yarn is traceable to California businessman Ray Dimmick. Early in 1950, the Los Angeles *Herald & Express* reported that Dimmick had discovered the wreckage of a saucer and its lifeless pilot on a mountainside in Mexico. While most early crash reports were proved to be hoaxes, they established physical attributes of saucer occupants that have persisted: a small humanoid physique and an oversized hairless head with prominent eyes.

STARTLING STORIES (June '52, opposite). FANTASTIC UNIVERSE (June '57, top). AMAZING STORIES (Feb. '58, left). ASTOUNDING (Sept. '58, center). FANTASTIC UNIVERSE (Feb. '58, right).

"ONLY WHEN we have to fight to stay human do we realize how precious it is."—*The Invasion of the Body Snatchers* (1956). Through the '50s and '60s, Americans felt unseen forces threatening their way of life. An outgrowth of commie infiltration paranoia, this fear found its way into science fiction television and film, often in the form of alien possession.

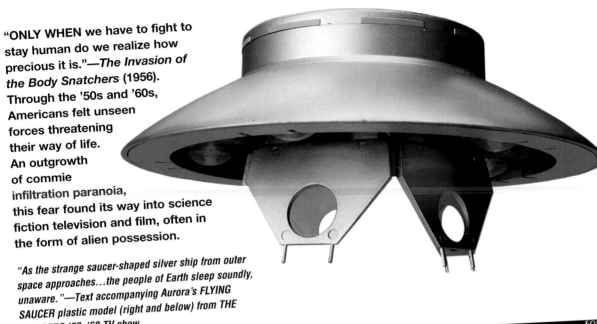

"As the strange saucer-shaped silver ship from outer space approaches…the people of Earth sleep soundly, unaware."—Text accompanying Aurora's FLYING SAUCER plastic model (right and below) from THE INVADERS '67–'68 TV show.

FLYING SAUCER
of "The Invaders"

AURORA

THE INVADERS

**Dam
of
Death**

Authorized Edition

Created
by
Larry Cohen

Main character David Vincent tried to warn a skeptical world of the alien infiltrators' insidious plans in each episode of THE INVADERS TV series, as well as in spin-off books and comics.

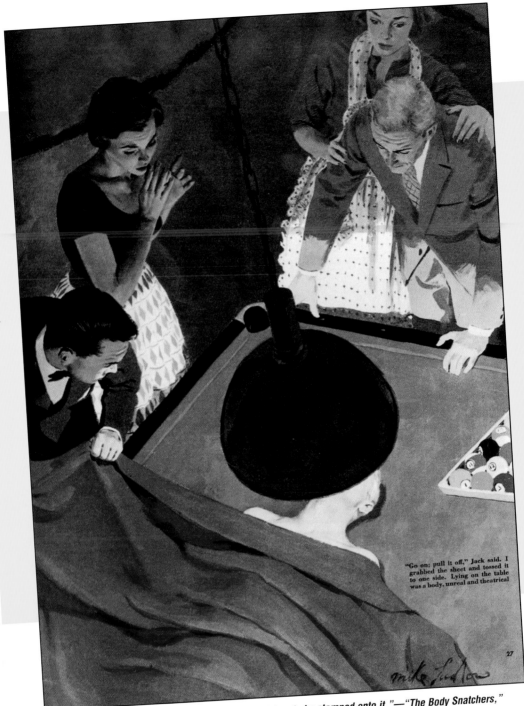

"Go on; pull it off," Jack said. I grabbed the sheet and tossed it to one side. Lying on the table was a body, unreal and theatrical

27

"It's like a blank face, waiting for the final finished face to be stamped onto it."—"The Body Snatchers," COLLIER'S, Nov. 26, '54. The illustration, by Mike Ludlow, is from the same issue.

"Then something moist touched my neck and I fainted."—Robert A. Heinlein's THE PUPPET MASTERS (GALAXY, Sept.– Nov. '51) is considered a superior treatment of the alien possession theme.

UNCLE IRA WASN'T UNCLE IRA!

"THERE WAS *no emotion*…only the memory and pretense of it." Pods from space take over in Jack Finney's *The Body Snatchers* (*Collier's*, Nov. 26–Dec. 24, '54). When people sleep their bodies are duplicated and their identities are absorbed. The novel and the film, *The Invasion of the Body Snatchers* (1956), both reflect the paranoia of the '50s and warn that humanity can be easily lost if it is not cherished and protected.

Alien parasites exert total mental and physical control over their human hosts in THE PUPPET MASTERS, an antecedent to Jack Finney's THE BODY SNATCHERS. The Dell First Edition paperback (1955, right) is an expanded version of the COLLIER'S serial.

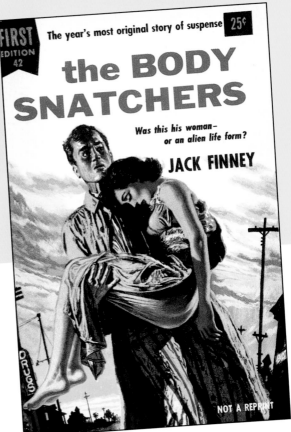

MASS INVASION OF THE WO

an unearthly
enemy defying
modern science
in a war
to-the-death!

INVISIBL
INV

Co-starring

JOHN AGAR · J!

with PHILIP TONGE · RO

Written by SAMUEL NEWMAN · Direct

A PREMIUM PICTURES,

At the height of the Cold War, Nikita Khrushchev said, "We will bury you!" The INVISIBLE INVADERS (1959, above) will "dig you up" to create a conquering horde of zombies in this precursor to NIGHT OF THE LIVING DEAD (1968). THE SPACE CHILDREN (1958, opposite bottom) features a space brain whose atypical motives are partly altruistic. It uses telepathic mind control to influence the children of rocket scientists to sabotage the launch of a nuclear rocket it regards as a threat to Earthkind and spacekind alike.

LD!

ADERS

N BYRON

T HUTTON · JOHN C

DWARD L. CAHN · Produced

resentation · Released thru UNIT

In John Wyndham's novel, THE MIDWICH CUCKOOS (1957), re-titled VILLAGE OF THE DAMNED (1960, below), children of otherworldly origin and abilities menace humanity.

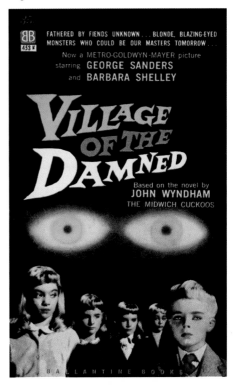

FATHERED BY FIENDS UNKNOWN . . . BLONDE, BLAZING-EYED
MONSTERS WHO COULD BE OUR MASTERS TOMORROW . . .

Now a METRO-GOLDWYN-MAYER picture
starring GEORGE SANDERS
and BARBARA SHELLEY

VILLAGE OF THE DAMNED

Based on the novel by
JOHN WYNDHAM
THE MIDWICH CUCKOOS

BALLANTINE BOOKS

PARAMOUNT PRESENTS

THE SPACE CHILDREN

STARRING MICHEL RAY · ADAM WILLIAMS · PEGGY WEBBER
PRODUCED BY WILLIAM ALLAND · DIRECTED BY JACK ARNOLD · SCREENPLAY BY BERNARD C. SCHOENFELD

MOVIES, TELEVISION, and sci-fi stories frequently portrayed saucer creatures as monstrous THINGS and ITS, as inhuman entities bent on violent subjugation or destruction of the human race. *The Thing From Another World* (1951) was loosely based on John W. Campbell Jr.'s eerie tale of paranoia, *Who Goes There?* Is your companion human or a shape-shifting, flesh-eating fiend? The movie substitutes some of the novel's paranoia with an increased sense of Cold War tension by relocating the action to a remote Alaskan base near the Russian border. A mysterious crashed object is investigated because of its possible Soviet origin.

An accurate rendition of Campbell's "Thing" (bottom right) appeared in FAMOUS MONSTERS' (June '61) abridged version of WHO GOES THERE? (Above) The 1951 edition of the book.

Galaxy
SCIENCE FICTION

APRIL 1956

35¢

Let's Build An Extraterrestrial! by Willy Ley

GALAXY's April '56 cover promises more than the article "Let's Build an Extraterrestrial!" delivers.

Detail of half sheet movie poster for INVASION OF THE SAUCER-MEN.

THE SAUCER CRAZE of the '50s inspired numerous flying saucer and space invasion films. But none had depicted a classic "little man" saucer occupant until *Invasion of the Saucer-Men* (1957). Designer Paul Blaisdell's wonderfully grotesque costumes had huge heads with bulging eyes and were fitted to dwarf actors. Outside of Blaisdell's Martians, the poster art (left) is the best thing about the movie—except the Saucer-Men are too big!

Saucer-Men admiring Detroit's space-age engineering (top). Some highly specialized actors had to take on part-time work after Hollywood lost interest in saucer movies (above).

EARTH VS. THE FLYING SAUCERS (1956) is *the* flying saucer movie of the '50s. Based on elements from Maj. Donald Keyhoe's *Flying Saucers From Outer Space (*1953), it has an air of authenticity lacking in other saucer films of the period. Besides *The War of the Worlds* (1953), *Earth Vs.* is the only full-scale saucer invasion film to spin out of Hollywood in the '50s. It is also one of the few sci-fi films to deliver on the promise of its poster. Washington, D.C., is totally destroyed by saucers—at movie's end few landmarks are left intact!

"When an armed and threatening power lands uninvited in our capitol, we don't meet it with tea and cookies."
—EARTH VS. THE FLYING SAUCERS (1956)

The film's flying saucers are the period's most convincing. They were brought to life by effects wizard Ray Harryhausen—"I still have an open mind about the subject and am eagerly waiting for more concrete evidence of their existence."

THE MYSTERIANS, *originally slated for U.S. release in 1958 by RKO, was distributed by MGM in 1959. Known as* CHIKYU BOEIGUN (1957) *in Japan, the film was Toho's first wide screen production. It was also their first "alien invasion" movie.*

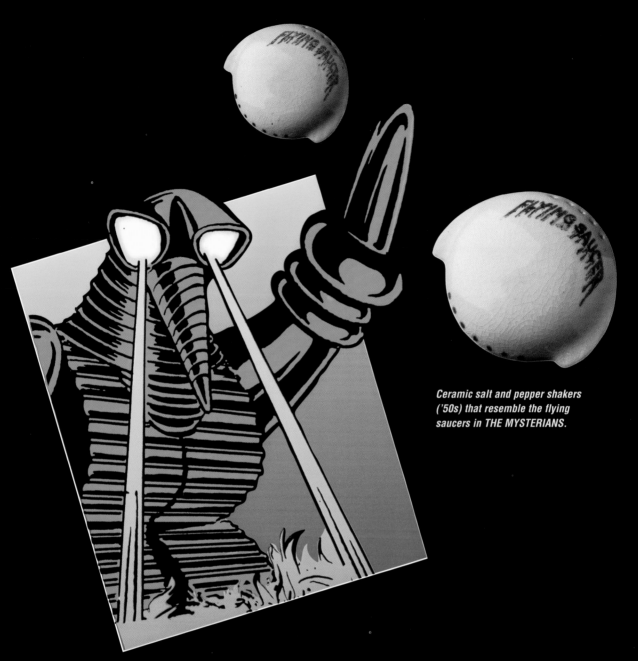

Ceramic salt and pepper shakers ('50s) that resemble the flying saucers in THE MYSTERIANS.

THE MYSTERIANS need women—and most of Japan too! A giant robot flashes death and destruction! Flying saucers blast jets! Entire cities wiped out! An invading hive of saucer aliens! Earth's armies united in a titanic battle! Preferring massive destruction to Hollywood's less costly "alien possession" theme, Toho's formula for *The Mysterians* became the studio's standard prescription for alien invasion films.

TERROR FROM OUTER SPACE!

THE 27th DAY

starring
GENE BARRY · VALERIE FRENCH

with

GEORGE VOSKOVEC · ARNO
STEFAN SCHNABE

Screen Play by JOHN MAN

Executive Producer—LEWIS J. RACH

PICTURE

THE 27th DAY
A COLUMBIA PICTURE

"OUR SUPERIOR. Our superior in every way."—*The Thing.* Many '50s films explore human reactions to "superior" aliens. These beings are often portrayed adhering to a code of ethics that doesn't necessarily reflect humanity's best interests. The book *The Flying Saucers Are Real* (1950) likens these aliens to explorers encountering primitive cultures.

In THE 27TH DAY (1957, left), aliens give humanity the power to destroy itself so they can move in. Turns out, only Reds are affected by the doomsday devices. Ad mat from THE COSMIC MAN (1959, above)—the alien who came to halt atomic development. There are many parallels between this movie and THE DAY THE EARTH STOOD STILL (1951).

STREAKING OUT OF THE UNKNOWN
COMES A STRANGE NEW TERROR!

THE FLYING SAUCER

Starring
Mikel Conrad · Pat Garrison · Lester Sharpe
Hantz Von Teuffen · Russell Hicks
Frank Darien

Produced and Directed By MIKEL CONRAD · Associate Producer MORRIS M. WEIN
Original Story By MIKEL CONRAD · Screen Adaptation By HOWARD IRVING YOUNG
A COLONIAL PRODUCTIONS PICTURE · *Released by* FILM CLASSICS, INC.

THE FLYING SAUCER (1950) was the first movie to describe UFOs as "flying saucers." The saucer was made on Earth and is almost acquired by the evil Russians in this early Red Scare flick. *UFO* (1954) was billed as a documentary treatment of "the truth about flying saucers." Captain Edward J. Ruppelt of Project Blue Book appears as himself in the film. Many of the incidents were based on information he provided. Most of the "actual" UFO footage in the film is poorly shot and it is hard to distinguish any saucers.

Poster of THE FLYING SAUCER (above). UFO pressbook cover and interior images featuring Capt. Thomas Mantell's fatal UFO incident (right, opposite left, opposite bottom). UFO lobbycard (opposite top).

"It appears to be a metallic object of tremendous size... I'm trying to close in on it!"

~and then he crashed!

For The First Time!
THE TRUTH ABOUT FLYING SAUCERS!

YOU WILL SEE THEM WITH YOUR OWN EYES!
Actual color films of the Unidentified Flying Objects that have been kept "top secret" until now!

EVERY SHOCKING WORD, EVERY FANTASTIC SCENE, EVERY FRIGHTENING MOMENT IS TRUE!

UFO
UNIDENTIFIED **F**LYING **O**BJECTS

CLARENCE GREENE and RUSSELL ROUSE present

Written by FRANCIS MARTIN · Produced by CLARENCE GREENE · Directed by WINSTON JONES · Released thru United Artists   With the people who actually lived the story of U.F.O.

During the latter half of the 19th century, numerous accounts told of huge, luminous wheels skimming just below the ocean surface, occasionally rising above the waters and disappearing into the night sky. In THE ATOMIC SUBMARINE (1960, right) the crew of a nuclear sub must save the world from a saucer hidden beneath the polar ice cap. The cover of GALAXY (Dec. '58, below) is a fanciful rendition of aqua-saucers exploring the depths of "the strange planet next door."

"OUR FLEET OF ATOMIC SU

...The shocking news that flames Tomorrow's War under the Arctic Ice!

COUNT DOWN for TERROR as the world's first Underwater Ballistics Missile is fired from under the NORTH POLE!

THE

ATOM

STS PICTURE starring

R FRANZ · DICK FORAN

HALSEY With JOI LANSING

Y · BOB STEELE · VICTOR VARCONI

NWAY as Sir Ian Hunt

In Association With   Co-Producer
JACK RABIN and IRVING BLOCK · HENRY SCHRAGE
        Directed by   Written by
PTON · SPENCER G. BENNET · ORVILLE H. HAMPTON
NG BLOCK and LOUIS DeWITT · ALEXANDER LASZLO PRODUCTION

Screen's Spectacular Infer

88

CELLULOID SAUCERS

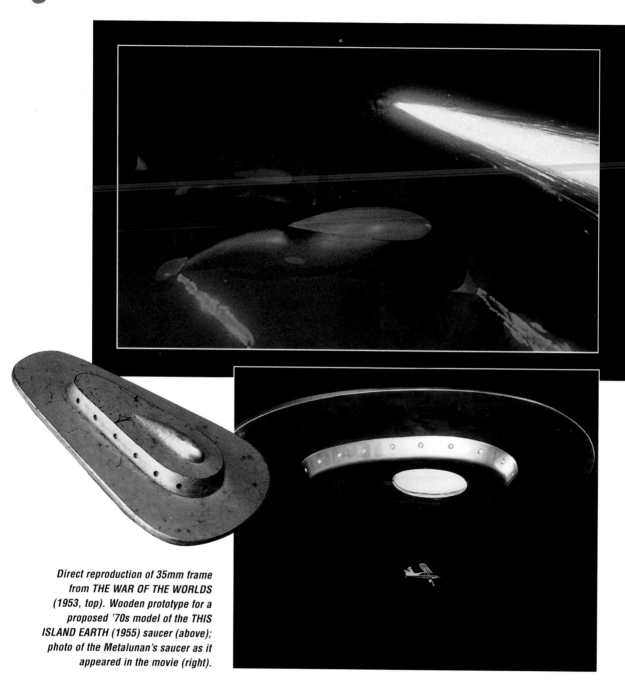

Direct reproduction of 35mm frame from THE WAR OF THE WORLDS (1953, top). Wooden prototype for a proposed '70s model of the THIS ISLAND EARTH (1955) saucer (above); photo of the Metalunan's saucer as it appeared in the movie (right).

A 1443

BANTAM BOOKS 35¢

W. J. STUART

FORBIDDEN PLANET

The story of man's leap to the stars and the astonishing discovery of a more than human wisdom—a power that could shatter our universe

Direct reproduction of 35mm frame from FORBIDDEN PLANET (1956, top). 1956 paperback based on the movie screenplay (far left). Metal, wind-up "Robbie" toy robot (Japan, '50s, left).

25¢

SUPER SCIENCE STORIES

A POPULAR PUBLICATION

JUNE

READ IT TODAY—LIVE IT TOMORROW!

A STORY OF
WORLDS BEYOND
EARTHMAN,
BEWARE!
by
POUL ANDERSON
MANY OTHERS

10 THE SKYSCRAPER TUMBLES

17 BEAST AND THE BEAUTY

19 BURNING FLESH

7 DESTROYING THE BRIDGE

"SCREAMING HYSTERICALLY, the people had no way of escaping."—*Mars Attacks* (no. 7, 1963). Stuffed in back pockets and hidden in homework assignments across America, the bloody rampages of ruthless Martians brought illicit delight to kids everywhere. Drawing from a history of graphic bubblegum cards—including *Horrors of War* (1938), *Red Menace* (1951), *Civil War News* (1962), and others—the onslaught of Topps' *Mars Attacks* topped them all. The 55 card set was eventually pulled off the market at the urging of parent groups. But not before schoolboys had gotten their fill of "Burning Flesh," "Burning Cattle," people "Crushed to Death," and an "Army of Insects." The set exploits every sci-fi and pulp convention: disintegration rays; giant bugs; imperiled women; and grotesque, big-brained, little alien marauders.

MARS ATTACKS owes a lot to pulp invasion clichés and borrows from scenes like that on the cover of SUPER SCIENCE STORIES (June '51, opposite). Evil invaders gleefully destroy all that is valued on Earth in typical MARS ATTACKS fashion (left).

IMAGINATION
FEBRUARY, 1953
35¢
STORIES OF SCIENCE AND FANTASY

...EARTH ALERT
BY KRIS NEVILLE

IMAGINATION
DECEMBER, 1955
35¢
SCIENCE FICTION
THE DAY
THE SUN DIED
By Daniel F. Galouye

IMAGINATION
FEBRUARY, 1958
35¢
SCIENCE FICTION
THE COSMIC LOOTERS
by Alexander Blade

IMAGINATION
AUGUST, 1953
35¢
STORIES OF SCIENCE AND FANTASY
THE BUTTONED SKY
by Geoff St. Reynard

IMAGINATION ALERT!!!

IMAGINATION was started by Ray Palmer in October 1950. He sold his ownership after only two issues. During its eight-year run, *Imagination* had more than its fair share of flying saucer and alien invasion covers. In this way, it managed to retain a bit of the old saucerian's charm.

"'Soon, now,' the mutants told each other with growing excitement, 'we shall go down and kill them.'"—"Earth Alert!" by Kris Neville (IMAGINATION, Feb. '53, opposite top left).

FANTASTIC STORY MAGAZINE

featuring:
ISLAND IN THE SKY by Manly Wade Wellman
HYPERPELOSITY by L. Sprague de Camp
STOLEN CENTURIES by Otis Adelbert Kline
EXPERIMENT by Roscoe Clark
THE MAN WHO LOOKED LIKE STEINMETZ by Robert Moore Williams

SEPT. 25¢

A THRILLING PUBLICATION

ALEX SCHOMBURG

ABDUCTED!

Beginning — COSMIC KILL — 2-part serial of thundering impact
AMAZING STORIES
APRIL 35¢
THE MAN WHO COLLECTED WOMEN—
The Most Shocking Hobby in the Universe

CONTACTEES like George Adamski and Buck Nelson willingly jumped aboard when they allegedly encountered saucer occupants. Others claimed to have been forced aboard. In one of the first reports of this type, Antonio Villas Boas, a Brazilian farmer, told of being captured by short humanoid creatures in 1957. He claimed he was stripped, medically examined, and forced to have sex with a beautiful alien female! Upon release, Villas Boas needed medical attention for cuts and radiation poisoning. No less interesting is the better known, prototypical abduction tale of Betty and Barney Hill. Regressive hypnosis brought out the details of their supposed abduction. The Hills claim to have been stopped by a saucer while driving down a deserted road. They were then brought aboard the ship and medically examined before being released. The grey-skinned, telepathic aliens with large eyes described by the Hills during one hypnosis session were very similar to an alien that appeared on *The Outer Limits* a few nights before. The abduction idea is old—medieval lore is full of tales about those detained in fairy circles and of midnight rapes by demonic incubi. Some believe these stories and abduction reports can be explained as hypnagogic dreams—hallucinations that occur during the groggy state between waking and sleep. But to abductees, their experiences are real and distressing.

"Human beings were nothing more than breeding animals."—(AMAZING STORIES, April '57, left). FANTASTIC STORY, Sept. '55 (top left).

THE MAGAZINE OF
Fantasy and Science Fiction

35¢ NOVEMBER

EVERY STORY
in this issue NEW

THEODORE STURGEON's
Brilliant new short novel
THE [WIDGET],
THE [WADGET],
AND BOFF

a Hoka novelet by
POUL ANDERSON and GORDON R. DICKSON
also
IDRIS SEABRIGHT   LEE CORREY   FRANK GRUBER

EMSH

Goblin-like little men combine extraterrestrial and faerie mythos (Nov. '54).

HORDES OF ATTACKING aliens menace the Earth in this gallery of invasion covers that play to the interest in saucers and the fear of losing the American way of life. Many of these covers have no relation to the stories or articles inside. They merely served as eye-catchers.

Both pages, clockwise from top: WORLDS OF TOMORROW (Nov. '66), FANTASTIC UNIVERSE (May '56, July '54, May '58, July '55), MENACE OF THE SAUCERS (1969), BEYOND THE SPECTRUM (1967).

FANTASTIC UNIVERSE SCIENCE FICTION

MAY 35c

SATAN ON HOLIDAY
by Ralph Bennitt

THE IVORY TOWER
by Milton Lesser

A QUESTION OF TIME
by Edmund Cooper

FANTASTIC UNIVERSE SCIENCE FICTION

An Astounding Story of Today's Science Brings Earth Into
Startling Conflict With the Alien Mission of . . .

THE MAN FROM THE FLYING SAUCER
by Sam Merwin Jr.

FANTASTIC UNIVERSE SCIENCE FICTION

NOW 35c
JULY

MARGARET ST. CLAIR · LESTER DEL REY · F. L. WALLACE
PHILIP JOSE FARMER · FRANK BELKNAP LONG · ALGIS BUDRYS
SAM CARSON · IDRIS SEABRIGHT · JOHN VICTOR PETERSON
ALL STORIES IN THIS ISSUE BRAND NEW

FANTASTIC UNIVERSE SCIENCE FICTION

FEATURING
BAIT FOR THE TIGER
A New Novel by LEE CHAYTOR

WE'LL NEVER CATCH THEM by IVAN T. SANDERSON

NEEDED—SPACE INTELLIGENCE by LESTER DEL REY

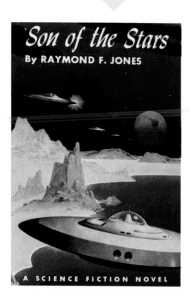

Son of the Stars
By RAYMOND F. JONES

A SCIENCE FICTION NOVEL

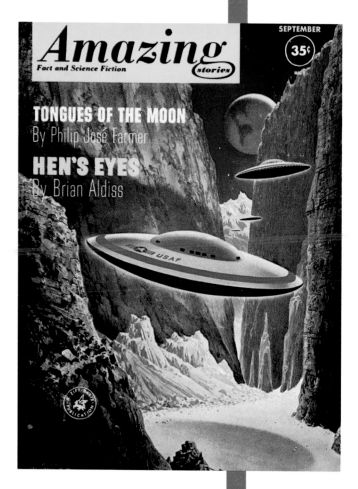

SEPTEMBER

Amazing stories

Fact and Science Fiction

35¢

TONGUES OF THE MOON
By Philip José Farmer

HEN'S EYES
By Brian Aldiss

DEC. 35¢

FANTASTIC **UNIVERSE** SCIENCE FICTION

IRVING E. COXE, JR. • JOHN WYNDHAM • RODGER DEE
THEODORE PRATT • HAL ELLSON • EVELYN E. SMITH
DAL STIVENS • RICHARD MATHESON • POUL ANDERSON
ALL STORIES IN THIS ISSUE BRAND NEW

Humans become the saucer pilots when Earthlings spread to the stars as predicted by science fiction magazines. "The voyage had lasted for hundreds of years, and the crew, and their grandparents, had never set foot on a planet's soil."—ORBIT (no. 1, '53, opposite). AMAZING STORIES (Sept. '61, above) and FANTASTIC UNIVERSE (Dec. '54, left). Anticipating humanity's exploration of the galaxy, aliens intend to obliterate mankind to prevent its spread into the universe in SON OF THE STARS (1952, top left).

ORBIT

SCIENCE FICTION

ANC

No. 1   35¢

NINE EXCITING STORIES
PLUS
Full-Length Novelette by
RICHARD ENGLISH

August Derleth, Mack Reynolds, Charles Beaumont, Paul Brandts

"YOU WILL FIND records of our presence in the mysterious symbols of ancient Egypt, where we made ourselves known in order to accomplish certain ends."—"Son of the Sun," (*Fantastic Adventures,* Nov. '47, opposite). Early reference to extraterrestrial intervention in Earth's past can be found in the writings of Charles Fort. The concept was later developed by Morris K. Jessup in his book, *The Case for the UFO* (1955), which suggested that flying saucers have been influencing humankind for thousands of years.

Man, did they let this thing go…. That's the last time we're helping anybody build a monument! (AMAZING STORIES, Dec. '57, top). Reminiscent of the final scene in PLANET OF THE APES (1968) are two covers by Alex Schomburg that appeared almost eleven years apart. The first was for FANTASTIC UNIVERSE (Aug./ Sept. '53, bottom right) and the second was for AMAZING STORIES (Feb. '64, bottom left) illustrating "The Golden Door."—"Earth was dead, but liberty still held her torch aloft."

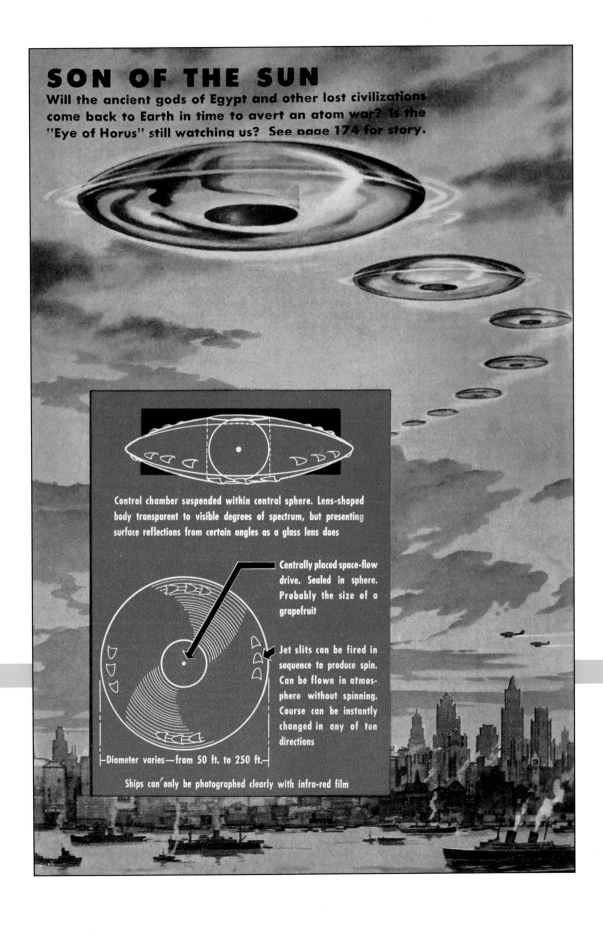

SON OF THE SUN

Will the ancient gods of Egypt and other lost civilizations come back to Earth in time to avert an atom war? Is the "Eye of Horus" still watching us? See page 174 for story.

Control chamber suspended within central sphere. Lens-shaped body transparent to visible degrees of spectrum, but presenting surface reflections from certain angles as a glass lens does

Centrally placed space-flow drive. Sealed in sphere. Probably the size of a grapefruit

Jet slits can be fired in sequence to produce spin. Can be flown in atmosphere without spinning. Course can be instantly changed in any of ten directions

—Diameter varies—from 50 ft. to 250 ft.—

Ships can only be photographed clearly with infra-red film

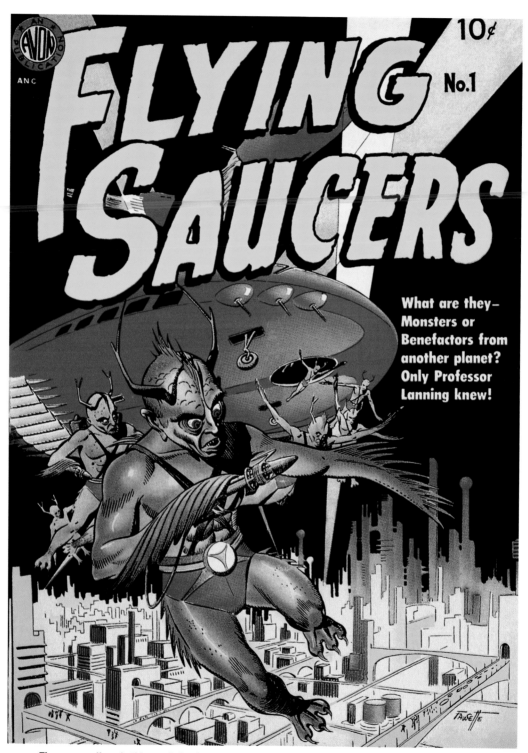

The saucer aliens in this comic book are really Earth's first inhabitants. They awaken from an eons-long sleep to prevent the world from destroying itself with nuclear weapons, as they had in the distant past (FLYING SAUCERS, no. 1, '50).

Vic Torry is victorious over the evil Szzz of Mercury in this "one shot" saucer epic from the publisher of Donald Keyhoe's paperback, THE FLYING SAUCERS ARE REAL (1950)—VIC TORRY AND HIS FLYING SAUCER (no. 1, 1950).

"The flying saucer is mass hysteria brought about by post-war insecurity and economic anxiety! It is obviously a pathological illusion aggravated by continuous publicity given it by press, radio, and comic books."—WEIRD SCIENCE (July–Aug. '50 reprint, left). WEIRD SCIENCE (Nov.-Dec. '52 reprint, below) features Wally Wood's version of diminutive, gooey-brained aliens. EC's FLYING SAUCER REPORT (Dec. '54 reprint, opposite).

CLASSIC SAUCERS IN CLASSIC COMICS

IN THE '50s and '60s all you could ever want to know about flying saucers could be had for a dime! EC Comics was one of the first to publish comics featuring flying saucers, producing a special *Flying Saucer Report* challenging the government: "What we have done here is attempted to show the inconsistencies and incongruities of the Air Force's wavering attitude toward this perplexing problem." The comic featured actual cases based on information supplied by Donald Keyhoe. Among the cases were three Keyhoe classics: the Mantell case, the Gorman case, and the Washington, D.C., cases. All involved experienced airmen, and in the Gorman and Washington, D.C., incidents, the UFOs had radar confirmation. In all three cases, Keyhoe, Ruppelt, and independent experts found the official Air Force explanations inadequate. EC continued to explore saucers, in both factual and fictional style, until they stopped publishing in February 1956.

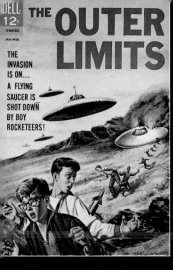

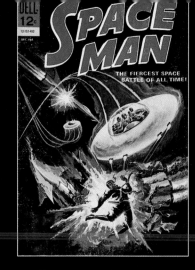

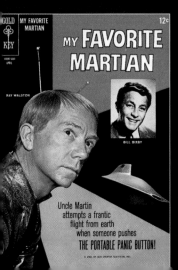

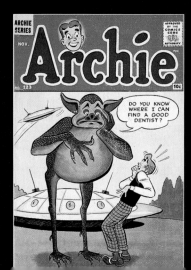

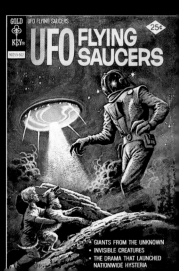

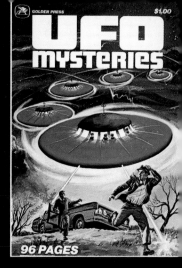

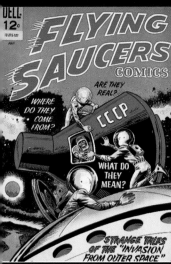

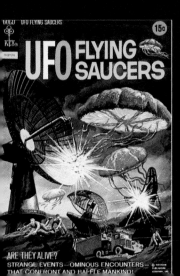

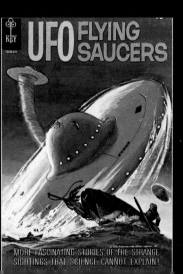

SCI-FI AND UFO storylines struggled as the '60s wore on. Some managed to survive—like *UFO Flying Saucers*, which lasted into the mid '70s with several reprint issues that featured earlier stories.

A selection of '60s and early '70s saucer comics.

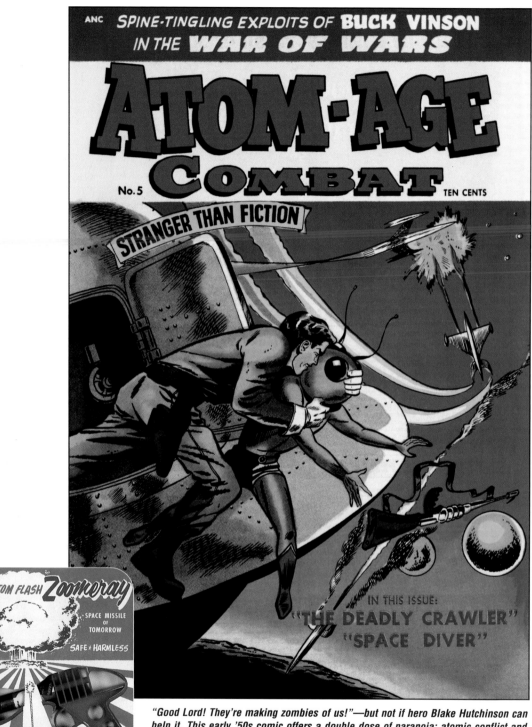

ATOM-AGE COMBAT No. 5

ANC SPINE-TINGLING EXPLOITS OF **BUCK VINSON** IN THE **WAR OF WARS**

ATOM-AGE COMBAT TEN CENTS

STRANGER THAN FICTION

IN THIS ISSUE:
"THE DEADLY CRAWLER"
"SPACE DIVER"

ATOM FLASH **Zoomeray**
SPACE MISSILE OF TOMORROW
SAFE & HARMLESS
SHOOTS 5 FEET OR MORE
AUTOMATICALLY RELOADS ITSELF

"Good Lord! They're making zombies of us!"—but not if hero Blake Hutchinson can help it. This early '50s comic offers a double dose of paranoia: atomic conflict and totalitarian aliens. Maybe Blake could use an Atom Flash Zoomeray (1950s). Its telescoping metallic cone would be perfect for poking out large, alien eyes.

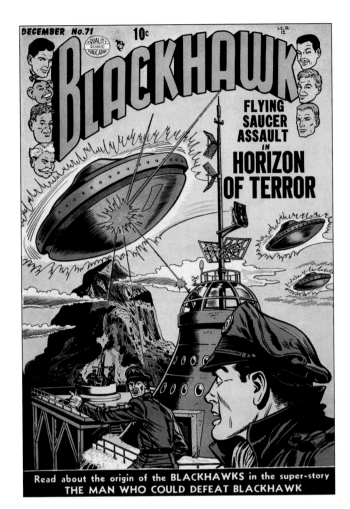

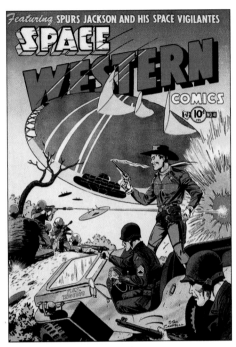

Taking a break from Nazis and commies, Blackhawk, ace freedom fighter, saves the world from becoming enslaved by yet another lost race of saucerites (no.71, 1953, left). Cattle rustlers were too easy, so Spurs and his pals switched formats for six issues to fight aliens (below).

The Navy's "flying Flapjack" didn't perform nearly as well as the X-36 in DON WINSLOW: FLYING SAUCER ATTACK! (no. 65, 1951, above left). Saucers were regular visitors in UNKNOWN WORLDS (no. 45, 1966, above right).

Swarms of tin wind-up and battery-operated flying saucers "made in Japan" invaded the American toy market in the '50s and '60s. A few inches to almost a foot in diameter...

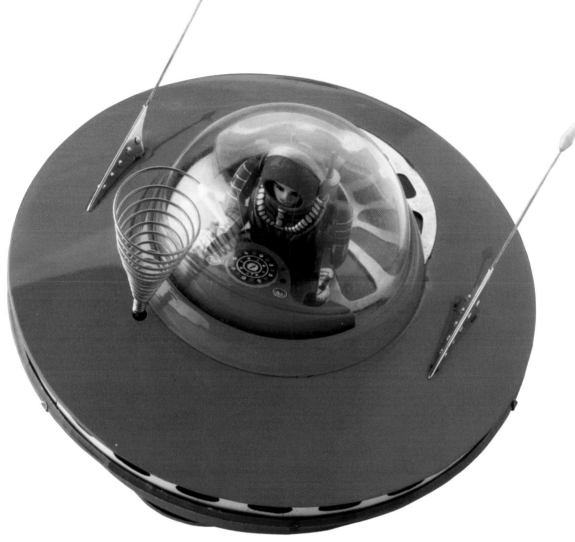

...these toys featured a variety of loud buzzes and whirs, blinking or spinning lights, and some type of Earth-bound bump-and-go "mystery action."

Several manufacturers produced similar "saucer guns" to take advantage of the '50s saucer craze. "Flies high and lands spinning." On the roof.

A jeweler's nerve and dad's hammer were required to extricate the friendly, sealed-in pilot of this gun's "Interplanetary patrol ship."

ATOMIC JET
FLYING·O·SAUCER
FORMIS PATENTED

KIDS, IT'S HERE! THE NEW MYSTERY ATOMIC-JET FLYING SAUCER

Watch it sail way up in the air—you can make it fly higher than a tall building — It will do five airplane stunts, too. Get several of them — and have FLYING SAUCER contests! Even Dads go crazy over it. Be the first in your neighborhood and amaze your friends. Atomic-Jet Flying Saucers and extra flying wheels on sale at

NEW! IMPROVED!

FLYING SAUCERS

The TOY THAT FIRES THE IMAGINATION

ZOOMS to AMAZING HEIGHTS— *Easy to Operate*

- *Colorful!*
- *Educational!*
- *Loaded with Sustained Play Value!*

THE TOY THAT ACTUALLY FLIES

IMPROVED 4-PIECE SET with 2 FLYING SAUCERS, ROTATING MOTOR HEAD, AND ACTUATING CORD!

79¢

SLIGHTLY HIGHER WEST OF DENVER

Passé helicopter toys of the '40s were hastily repackaged as flying saucer toys in the '50s. The rubber band launchers for the cardboard and plastic saucers (1960s, opposite) could also send hair pins and spit wads into orbit.

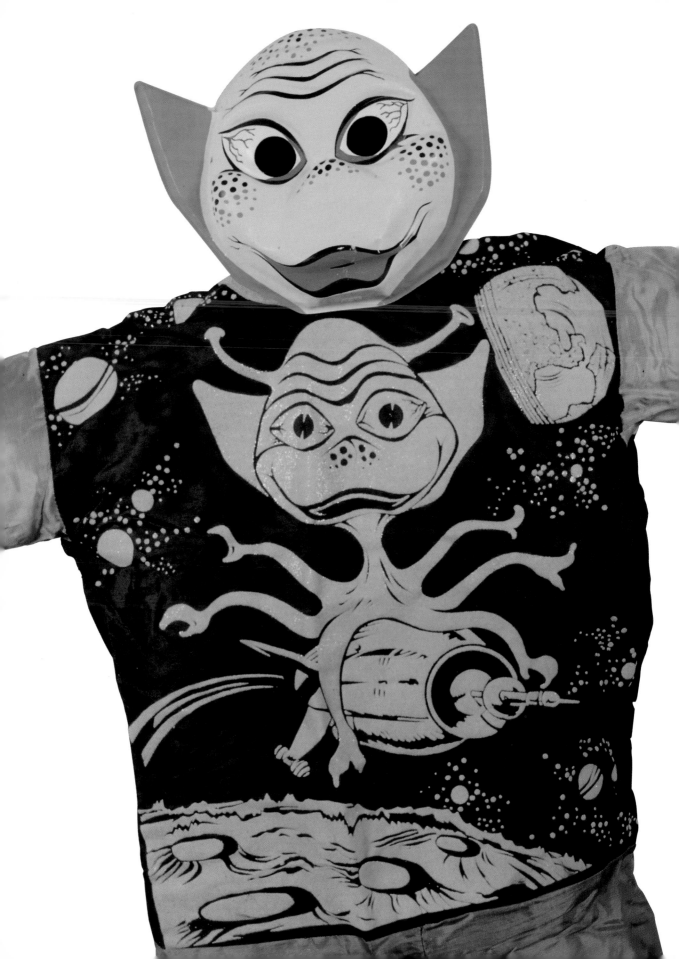

For a mere $1.59, you could be transformed into a Halloween space monster (opposite). The costume was manufactured in the mid '60s and its large "Saf-T-C Eyeholes" made it kin to the original saucer occupants reported in the early '50s. A flying saucer platform is used for treasure hunting among the asteroids in THE GRANDSTAND BOOK FOR BOYS ('50s, left).

STOP THE MARTIANS!

White in Rocket Ship Stops Attack

Jiggle **PUZZLE**
a game of skill

© 1957 Comon Tatar, Inc., Blasdell, N. Y.

Parents bought toys like the Jiggle Puzzle (1957, above) to occupy kids on long road trips—"Hey, watch those bumps...I'm trying to save the world back here!" Terrytoons' Deputy Dawg in "Bait From Outer Space" (1962, below)—color slides for home viewing from Kenner's "Give a Show" projector.

HEY, DEPUTY DAWG....
A FLYING SAUCER JUST LANDED!

LOOK, HERE THEY COME!

HEY, THAT'S JUST WHAT I NEED!

AND NOW FER THE CATBOYS!

Previously unpublished illustration by Jack Davis. A line art version was published in HUMBUG (Aug. '57)...

... "You'll stand guard... If anything strange happens call me at once!—What could happen!"